T012464

CREATIVE
•CROSSWORDS•

Published in 2022 by Welbeck

An Imprint of Welbeck Non-Fiction Limited, part of Welbeck
Publishing Group
20 Mortimer Street London W1T 3JW

First published by Carlton Books as *Pretty Puzzles: Crosswords*
in 2010

A CIP catalogue record for this book is available from the British
Library.

ISBN 978-1-78739-894-8

Printed in China

10 9 8 7 6 5 4 3 2 1

CREATIVE
·CROSSWORDS·

TEST YOURSELF WITH OVER
100 VARIED WORD PUZZLES

WELBECK

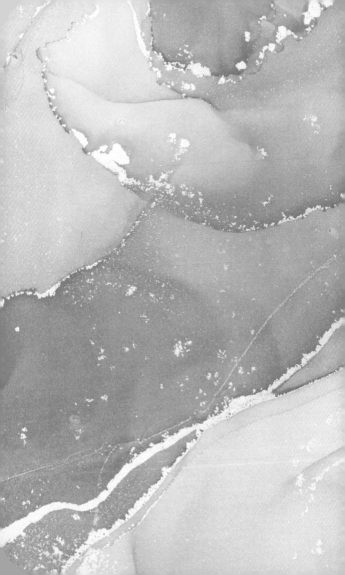

INTRODUCTION

Welcome to the wonderful world of puzzles!

This little book is packed full of challenging and engaging crossword puzzles of many different kinds. Although there are some traditional puzzles, there are many unusual variations to challenge your lexical-solving ability and keep you sharp as a tack!

Be sure to tackle our tricky anagram-based puzzles, specially designed to challenge your vocabulary and really exercise your brain.

All the following have been carefully selected to give you the most puzzle-solving pleasure possible, so have fun as you puzzle your way through the book, and look out for others in the series!

ALPHAFIT

Each of the 26 letters of the alphabet should be entered into the grid once, and only once.

A	B	C	D	E	F	G	H	I	J	K	L	M

N	O	P	Q	R	S	T	U	V	W	X	Y	Z

ACROSS

2 Modern watch crystal (6)
5 Groups of birds (6)
7 1950s dance style (4)

DOWN

1 Unbuttered (toast) (3)
3 Improvement, increase (7)
4 Rigid container (3)
6 Sewn edge (3)

QUICK CROSSWORD

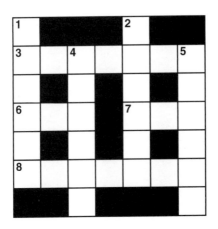

ACROSS
3 For very little expense (7)
6 Soccer official (3)
7 Black liquid mineral (3)
8 Imagined object of terror (7)

DOWN
1 Sacred Egyptian beetle (6)
2 Self-assurance (6)
4 Likeness of a figure (6)
5 Cowardly hue (6)

QUICK CROSSWORD

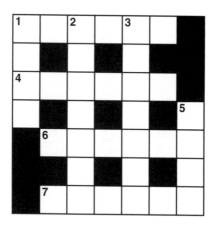

ACROSS

1 Serve (4,2)
4 Northern Asian medicine man (6)
6 Tending to leave greasy marks (6)
7 Gentle wind (6)

DOWN

1 Sundown (4)
2 Vocal hesitation (7)
3 In ignorance (7)
5 Burning pile of wood (4)

QUICK CROSSWORD

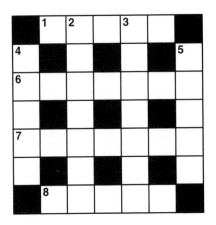

ACROSS
1 Hat or horse race (5)
6 Warehouse workers (7)
7 Eaten with cheese (7)
8 Liable to cry (5)

DOWN
2 Surrounded territory (7)
3 End a relationship (5,2)
4 Piquant substance (5)
5 High-interest moneylending (5)

QUICK CROSSWORD

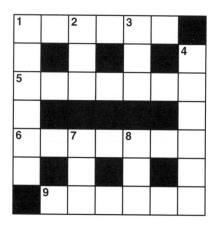

ACROSS
1 Crafty (6)
5 Long-armed apes (7)
6 Art of paper-folding (7)
9 Shout from the audience (6)

DOWN
1 Enlist (4,2)
2 Chest bone (3)
3 Go a-courting (3)
4 Have high hopes (6)
7 Anger (3)
8 Noah's craft (3)

ALPHAFIT

Each of the 26 letters of the alphabet should be
entered into the grid once, and only once.

A	B	C	D	E	F	G	H	I	J	K	L	M
N	O	P	Q	R	S	T	U	V	W	X	Y	Z

ACROSS
4 Assignments (4)
6 Soft, moldable (4)
7 Touched on each shoulder with
a sword (8)

DOWN
1 Mineral used in watches (6)
2 Common insect (3)
3 Mimic scornfully (4)
5 Turn around quickly (4)

QUICK CROSSWORD

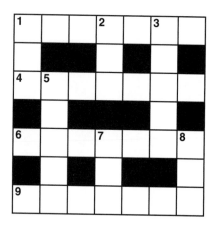

ACROSS
1 Body part to pierce (7)
4 Celebratory (7)
6 Behave without restraint or discipline (3,4)
9 Putting on (a play) (7)

DOWN
1 Mischievous supernatural being (3)
2 Fate, destiny (3)
3 Sloping edge (5)
5 Blow up (volcano) (5)
7 Toupee (3)
8 Turned over soil (3)

QUICK CROSSWORD

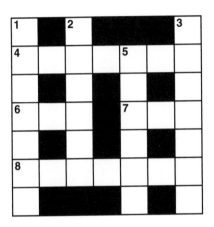

ACROSS
4 Vaporlike (7)
6 Only even prime number (3)
7 The lot (3)
8 Track down, look for (4,3)

DOWN
1 Self-love (7)
2 On dry land (6)
3 Keep in solitary confinement (7)
5 Skillful speaker (6)

QUICK CROSSWORD

ACROSS
1 Food thickener from seaweed (4)
5 Imaginary ideal country (6)
6 Spanish holiday or festival (6)
7 Biblical paradise (4)

DOWN
2 Alight or dismount (3,3)
3 Sated, full (7)
4 Fight, encounter (6)

QUICK CROSSWORD

ACROSS

3 Inflamed swelling on the big toe (6)

5 Uncomplaining (7)

6 Fourscore (6)

DOWN

1 Person who gives up easily (7)

2 Exhume (7)

4 Sugar coating (5)

MISFIT

25 out of 26 letters of the alphabet should be
entered into the grid once, and only once.
Can you tell which one is missing?

A	B	C	D	E	F	G	H	I	J	K	L	M
N	O	P	Q	R	S	T	U	V	W	X	Y	Z

ACROSS
4 Plane figure with six sides (7)
6 Peculiarity of behavior (5)
7 CIA agent (3)

DOWN
1 Pack of cards (4)
2 Door posts (5)
3 Very tall (5)
5 Namely, in brief (3)

QUICK CROSSWORD

ACROSS
1 Bowler-hatted Bond villain (6)
5 Relating to noise (5)
6 Push forward (5)
7 Auto shed (6)

DOWN
2 Stylish (7)
3 Berries used to flavor gin (7)
4 Accumulation of uncompleted work (7)

QUICK CROSSWORD

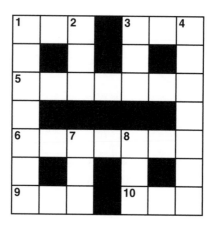

ACROSS

1 Handle clumsily (3)
3 Bridge call (3)
5 Subject to duty (7)
6 Type of bet (4–3)
9 Evergreen tree (3)
10 Jacob's son (3)

DOWN

1 Articles of baked clay (7)
2 Candle substance (3)
3 Front part of overalls (3)
4 Having an expression like Bambi's? (3–4)
7 Female whale (3)
8 Hair piece (3)

QUICK CROSSWORD

ACROSS
1 Meadow's main plant (5)
5 Decorative bottle (4,3)
6 A type of small guitar (7)
8 Furrow the brow (5)

DOWN
2 Regret (3)
3 Not fast (6)
4 Argue (6)
7 Litigation (3)

QUICK CROSSWORD

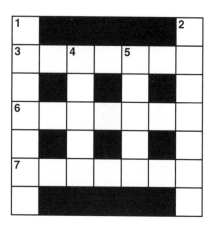

ACROSS

3 Inconsiderate driver (4,3)
6 Be subjected to (7)
7 Fortress protecting a town (7)

DOWN

1 Defeat decisively (7)
2 Dishonorable (7)
4 Examination of accounts (5)
5 Chartered (5)

ALPHAFIT

Each of the 26 letters of the alphabet should be entered into the grid once, and only once.

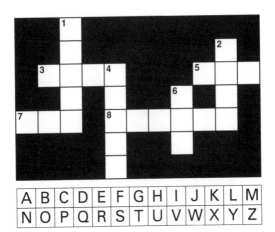

| A | B | C | D | E | F | G | H | I | J | K | L | M |
| N | O | P | Q | R | S | T | U | V | W | X | Y | Z |

ACROSS

3 Unruly groups (4)
5 Large, handled vessel (3)
7 ___ Do Fools Fall in Love?, Diana Ross single (3)
8 Lead-up to Christmas (6)

DOWN

1 Person who acts for another (5)
2 Give up on a task (4)
4 Far from strict (5)
6 A type of hat; city in Morrocco (3)

QUICK CROSSWORD

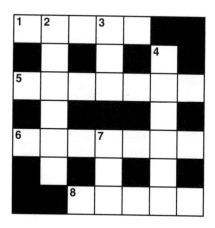

ACROSS
1 Reflection (in a mirror) (5)
5 Mollusk with a fan-shaped shell (7)
6 Ruling sovereigns (7)
8 Psychiatrist's sofa (5)

DOWN
2 Scale copy, dummy (4-2)
3 Hairstyling substance (3)
4 Fine French brandy (6)
7 In addition, as well (3)

MISFIT

25 out of the 26 letters of the alphabet should be
entered into the grid once, and only once.
Can you find which letter has not been used?

A	B	C	D	E	F	G	H	I	J	K	L	M
N	O	P	Q	R	S	T	U	V	W	X	Y	Z

ACROSS
4 Pavilion or summerhouse (**6**)
6 Parched (**3**)
7 Sudden notions (**5**)

DOWN
1 Picture playing cards (5)
2 Grassland of South Africa (5)
3 Wily (4)
5 Clever one-liner (4)

QUICK CROSSWORD

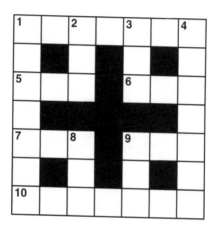

ACROSS
1 Construct once more (7)
5 Consume (3)
6 Instrument for unlocking (3)
7 Dull stupid fellow (3)
9 In days gone by (3)
10 Tight embrace (4,3)

DOWN
1 Long-stalked plant (7)
2 Busy buzzer! (3)
3 Ruffle the feathers of (3)
4 Throughout the hours of light (3-4)
8 Offshore waters (3)
9 Burned residue (3)

QUICK CROSSWORD

ACROSS
2 Money affairs (7)
5 Overnight protest (5-2)
6 Published issue (7)

DOWN
1 Of the nobility (6)
3 Watchful (5)
4 Earring for nonpierced ears (4-2)

QUICK CROSSWORD

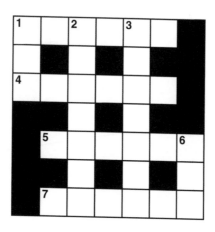

ACROSS

1 Piecrust (6)
4 Springy, pliant (6)
5 Be next to (6)
7 Saucy view (6)

DOWN

1 Chapel bench (3)
2 Long and slender (7)
3 Admonition (7)
6 Zero (3)

QUICK CROSSWORD

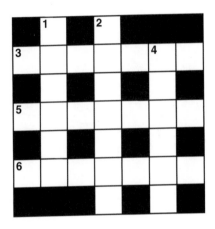

ACROSS
3 Highly seasoned (7)
5 Isolate (7)
6 Expertise (7)

DOWN
1 Straight (6)
2 Wild West bandits (7)
4 Practices nakedness (6)

QUICK CROSSWORD

ACROSS

4 Supported frames on wheels (7)

6 Dark, bituminous substance (3)

7 Friend (3)

8 Lend a hand (4,3)

DOWN

1 On edge (7)

2 More than one, grammatically (6)

3 Keep in solitary confinement (7)

5 Give someone a job (6)

QUICK CROSSWORD

ACROSS
1 Old (4)
5 Whiner (6)
6 Disquiet (6)
7 Inert gas (4)

DOWN
2 Reach a level of maturity (4,2)
3 Underground prison (7)
4 Very quick, in music (6)

QUICK CROSSWORD

ACROSS

3 Weight attached to a fishing line (6)

5 Two-pack card game (7)

6 Jaunty, dashing (6)

DOWN

1 Personal competition (7)

2 Barbaric (7)

4 Ability (5)

QUICK CROSSWORD

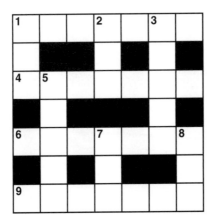

ACROSS
1 Dummy pill (7)
4 Reading desk (7)
6 Small sea fish (7)
9 Humiliated (7)

DOWN
1 Buddy (3)
2 Creature that has got your tongue (3)
3 Nobleman (5)
5 Fundamental character (5)
7 Infusion (3)
8 Supreme being, creator of the universe (3)

MISFIT

25 out of the 26 letters of the alphabet should be
entered into the grid once, and only once.
Can you find which letter has not been used?

| A | B | C | D | E | F | G | H | I | J | K | L | M |
| N | O | P | Q | R | S | T | U | V | W | X | Y | Z |

ACROSS

1 Sauté (3)
3 Pledging (8)
6 Bets on (a horse) (5)

DOWN

1 Something you can do to a
muscle (4)
2 Questions contest (4)
4 Electrical resistance units (4)
5 Chewing structure (3)

QUICK CROSSWORD

ACROSS
1 Large (3)
3 Knight's title (3)
5 Waltzing (7)
6 Wounded (7)
9 Choke (3)
10 Method (3)

DOWN
1 Sheets, blankets, etc. (7)
2 Revolver, for instance (3)
3 Move on snow (3)
4 Stiffly, inflexibly (7)
7 Large, handled vessel (3)
8 To propel with oars (3)

QUICK CROSSWORD

ACROSS
1 Having unusual tastes (5)
5 Knoll (7)
6 Color of the heavens (3-4)
8 Talk foolishly (5)

DOWN
2 Laid up (3)
3 Create or cause (a fuss) (4,2)
4 Basket material (6)
7 On the contrary (3)

QUICK CROSSWORD

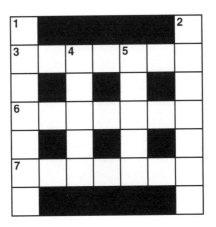

ACROSS

3 A West African tree (7)
6 Pleased, satisfied (7)
7 Cash put by (4,3)

DOWN

1 Run away (7)
2 Unusable leftovers (7)
4 Treats for the dog (5)
5 Water bird (5)

ALPHAFIT

Each of the 26 letters of the alphabet should be
entered into the grid once, and only once.

ACROSS
3 Satisfy (a thirst) (6)
4 Kill (by sci-fi laser) (3)
6 Be luminous (4)
7 Awkward situation (3)
8 Above the horizon (3)

DOWN
1 React in surprise (4)
2 Pounds, pulsates (6)
5 Fervent (4)

QUICK CROSSWORD

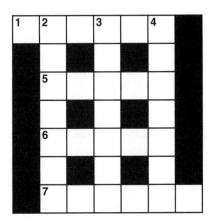

ACROSS
1 Funny TV show based on everyday life (6)
5 Frequent (5)
6 Join forces (5)
7 Sign on (6)

DOWN
2 Done on company premises (2-5)
3 Critical (7)
4 Parents (7)

MISFIT

25 of the 26 letters of the alphabet should be
entered into the grid once, and only once.
Can you find which letter has not been used?

ACROSS
5 Maple tree with
winged seeds (8)
6 Vitality (4)

DOWN
1 For what purpose? (3)
2 Plant from which linseed oil
is obtained (4)
3 Position in paid employment
(3)
4 Maintained (4)
5 Ink-squirting sea creature (5)

QUICK CROSSWORD

ACROSS
1 Choice steak (1-4)
5 Fan-shape edible shellfish (7)
6 Sly (7)
8 Digging implement (5)

DOWN
2 Give support to (4,2)
3 Zero (3)
4 Having antlers (6)
7 Pinch (3)

QUICK CROSSWORD

ACROSS
2 They work as sculptors (7)
5 Fierce wind (7)
6 Horse's tuft of hair (7)

DOWN
1 Persuade by flattery (6)
3 Record-making material (5)
4 Make smaller (6)

QUICK CROSSWORD

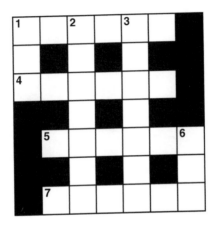

ACROSS
1 Second-in-command (6)
4 Riddle (6)
5 Caress (6)
7 A minor thing (6)

DOWN
1 Perish (3)
2 Dog used for hunting game (7)
3 Recreation period (4,3)
6 Organ of sight (3)

QUICK CROSSWORD

ACROSS

3 Paralyze with terror (7)
5 Feminine (7)
6 Slander (7)

DOWN

1 Hat with a curled brim (6)
2 Imagine (5,2)
4 Grave crime (6)

QUICK CROSSWORD

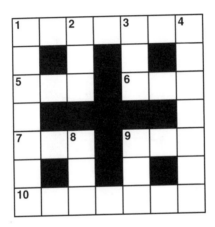

ACROSS
1 Part of a scrum (4,3)
5 Jazz band instrument (3)
6 Enclosed storage container (3)
7 Heavy mist (3)
9 Front part of a fire engine (3)
10 Pining, yearning (7)

DOWN
1 Modest (7)
2 Boating steersman (3)
3 Chafe (3)
4 Someone who rambles on (7)
8 Liquor flavoured with juniper (3)
9 T'ai ___, martial art (3)

ALPHAFIT

Each of the 26 letters of the alphabet should be
entered into the grid once, and only once.

| A | B | C | D | E | F | G | H | I | J | K | L | M |
| N | O | P | Q | R | S | T | U | V | W | X | Y | Z |

ACROSS

2 People in Gordon Ramsay's
profession (5)
5 Polish monetary unit (5)
6 Wet soil (3)
7 Triangular sail (3)

DOWN

1 To cause trouble (3)
2 Sob (3)
3 Brave woman? (5)
4 Elbowing (6)

QUICK CROSSWORD

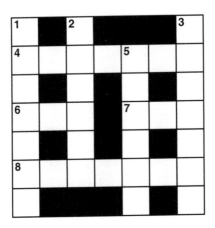

ACROSS

4 Stirring (7)
6 Small, collapsible bed (3)
7 Chum (3)
8 Ballroom dance (3-4)

DOWN

1 Nail to a cross (7)
2 Additional levy (6)
3 Suppleness (7)
5 Buy from abroad (6)

QUICK CROSSWORD

ACROSS
1 Guitar run (4)
5 Hooded pullover jacket (6)
6 Divulge (6)
7 Stomach-churning (4)

DOWN
2 Disregard (6)
3 Animal's front limb (7)
4 Person who slides over ice (6)

QUICK CROSSWORD

ACROSS
3 Old-style soccer forward (6)
5 Patella (7)
6 Spread in many directions (3,3)

DOWN
1 Ennoble (7)
2 Invent, imagine (5,2)
4 Concerned about the environment (5)

MISFIT

25 of the the 26 letters of the alphabet should be entered into the grid once, and only once. Can you find which letter has not been used?

A	B	C	D	E	F	G	H	I	J	K	L	M
N	O	P	Q	R	S	T	U	V	W	X	Y	Z

ACROSS
4 Male sponsor to an infant (9)
6 Wisecracks (5)

DOWN
1 Cut (grass) (3)
2 Sponsors (5)
3 Added tax (4)
5 Unlucky influence (4)

QUICK CROSSWORD

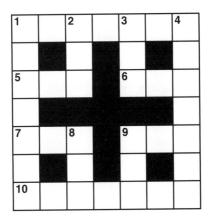

ACROSS

1 Dreamed (7)
5 Globe with a cross (3)
6 Opening device (3)
7 Old washing vessel (3)
9 In days gone by (3)
10 Cloth for washing dishes (7)

DOWN

1 Iced up (7)
2 Writing point of a pen (3)
3 Fluid used for writing (3)
4 From dawn until dusk (3-4)
8 Form of public transport (3)
9 We breathe it (3)

QUICK CROSSWORD

ACROSS

1 Mesh (3)
3 Cry (3)
5 Doing a foxtrot or a waltz (7)
6 Part of something (7)
9 Attain (3)
10 Soft leather (3)

DOWN

1 Soft substance used as stuffing (7)
2 Tight coil of hair (3)
3 Snow footwear item (3)
4 Narrow-minded (7)
7 Other than (3)
8 Sort, kind (3)

QUICK CROSSWORD

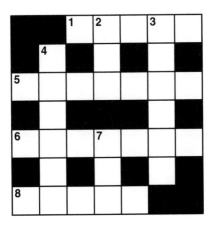

ACROSS
1 Rich pungent coffee (5)
5 Slot for a broadcast (7)
6 Armed robbery (5-2)
8 Hang in loose folds (5)

DOWN
2 On loan (3)
3 Middle Eastern dip (6)
4 Cold period of the year (6)
7 Policeman (3)

QUICK CROSSWORD

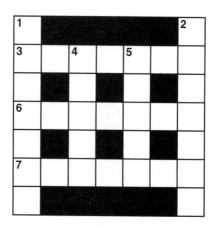

ACROSS

3 North African country (7)
6 Have a change of heart (7)
7 Muffling gadget (7)

DOWN

1 Make tidy (7)
2 Charge made for serving a customer's own wine (7)
4 Chopper blade (5)
5 Make cold (5)

QUICK CROSSWORD

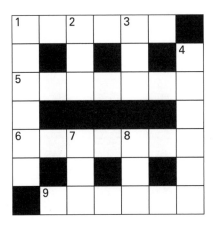

ACROSS
1 Scalawag (6)
5 Plume (7)
6 Rubs out (7)
9 Muscle-to-bone tissue (6)

DOWN
1 Roofing beam (6)
2 Offshore waters (3)
3 Smoker's flickings (3)
4 Jail (6)
7 Enemy (3)
8 Common seawater fish (3)

ANAGRID

Every answer is a new word formed from the letters used in the clue.

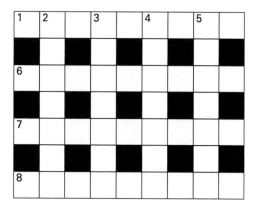

ACROSS
1 NIT AT ETON
6 SOME MOUNT
7 GREEN RAMS
8 PERSONATE

DOWN
2 WORTLES
3 PER GENE
4 I ATTAIN
5 PUT NOEL

ANAGRID

Every answer is a new word formed from the
letters used in the clue.

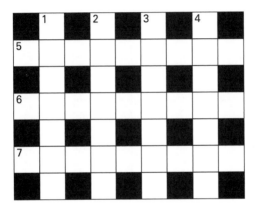

ACROSS
- **5** PEG IN MIND
- **6** DEALS HAND
- **7** ROM COMICS

DOWN
- **1** MAIN SEA
- **2** RUDE REV
- **3** DAVE CAN
- **4** DISSENT

NO BLANKS!

A crossword with no square wasted!

1	2	3	4
5			
6			
7			
8			
9			

ACROSS
1 Cut down
5 Operatic song
6 Placid
7 Tiny land mass
8 ___ Armstrong, astronaut
9 ___hound

DOWN
1 Directly opposite
2 Pencil-mark remover
3 ___ Langtry, famous actress
4 In a feeble way

QUICK CROSSWORD

ACROSS
1 Slander (6)
5 Contend (3)
6 Fish eggs (3)
7 Consume (3)
8 Mythical bird (3)
9 Little devil (3)
10 Casual top (1-5)

DOWN
1 Distract (6)
2 Overcharges (7)
3 Vermouth (7)
4 Tyrant (6)

BOX WISE

Can you put these three-letter groups into the
numbered boxes to produce twelve six-letter words?
Each of them will start in one box and finish
in another as indicated by an arrow.

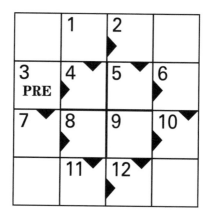

CER	CON	DOR
EAL	FAB	ION
ISE	LES	LIN
MER	PRE	STO

ANAGRID

Every answer is a new word formed from the letters used in the clue.

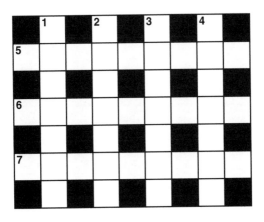

ACROSS

5 COAL PIPES
6 INTO A RITE
7 CRATE POLE

DOWN

1 PET RUST
2 THIS ORC
3 LIT SHOE
4 VOTE TAG

ANAGRID

Every answer is a new word formed from the
letters used in the clue.

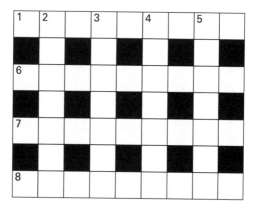

ACROSS
1 LATE TEAMS
6 ENTORPIUM
7 REED SOUND
8 TUTS AT TEE

DOWN
2 PETS MET
3 OUTLOOK
4 EAT MINE
5 GNAT NET

QUICK CROSSWORD

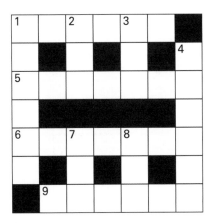

ACROSS

1 Select (6)
5 Seemingly suicidal rodent! (7)
6 Render unnecessary (7)
9 Rogues (6)

DOWN

1 Naive, inexperienced (6)
2 Unit of resistance (3)
3 Snowshoe (3)
4 Concurs (6)
7 Suction cleaner, abbreviated (3)
8 Give weapons to (3)

SO BE IT

With the help of "SO" in each answer,
can you complete the grid?

1	S	O				
2		S	O			
3			S	O		
4				S	O	
5					S	O
6						S	O

1 Witchcraft
2 Set apart
3 Stonework
4 Ugly sight
5 Spray can
6 Caribbean folk song

QUICK CROSSWORD

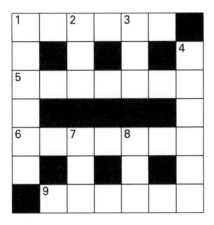

ACROSS
1 Fall headlong (6)
5 Bridal train (7)
6 Handled menacingly (7)
9 Excited activity (6)

DOWN
1 Hurled (6)
2 Judo flooring (3)
3 ___ Cariou, *Blue Bloods* actor (3)
4 Church usher (6)
7 Australian bird (3)
8 Tiny spot (3)

ANAGRID

Every answer is a word formed from
the letters in the clue.

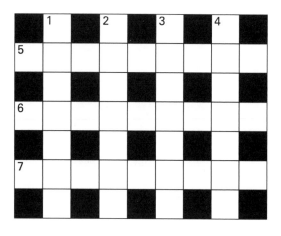

ACROSS
5 STRAP LINE
6 MICE ANTIC
7 SMART SAIL

DOWN
1 RILE CAT
2 REAP SAP
3 CAST IAN
4 TIE MADE

LIT UP

With the help of "LIT" in each line,
can you solve all the clues?

1				**L**	**I**	**T**
2			**L**	**I**	**T**	
3		**L**	**I**	**T**		
4	**L**	**I**	**T**			
5	**L**	**I**	**T**			

1 Glittering at night
2 Like WWII clothing?
3 Citizen army
4 Sparkle
5 Ritual service?

ANAGRID

Every answer is a new word formed from
the letters used in the clue.

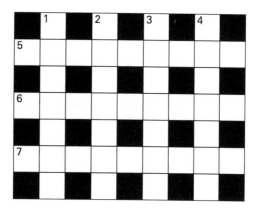

ACROSS
5 MINE FAILS
6 ICEMAN PAL
7 TIRE OR TRY

DOWN
1 BERATED
2 TRIPODS
3 TIDYING
4 ALLERGY

NO BLANKS!

A crossword with no square wasted!

¹	²	³	⁴
⁵			
⁶			
⁷			
⁸			
⁹			

ACROSS
1 Front part
5 Wild goat
6 Ghastly child
7 Bottom
8 Biblical paradise
9 Remainder

DOWN
1 Little liar!
2 Chafe
3 Discontinues
4 Scope, range

BOX WISE

Can you put these three-letter groups into the
numbered boxes to produce twelve six-letter words?
Each of them will start in one box and finish
in another as indicated by an arrow.

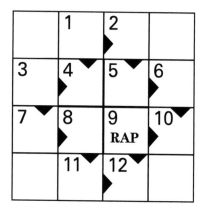

AIL	BEH	ENT
FUL	IND	ING
MEN	OLD	RAP
REF	TOR	USE

QUICK CROSSWORD

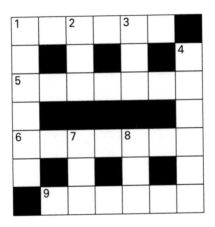

ACROSS

1 Dart, sprint (6)
5 Cruel (7)
6 Improve (7)
9 Surround completely (6)

DOWN

1 Replaced by another footballer? (6)
2 South of Canada (3)
3 Sewer dweller? (3)
4 Me personally! (6)
7 Farmyard bird (3)
8 Higher education institute in Washington, DC (inits) (3)

ANAGRID

Every answer is a word formed from the letters in the clue.

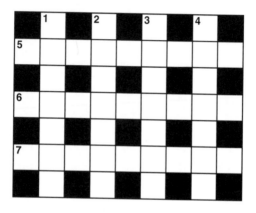

ACROSS

5 VISA IRONY
6 EGG IN TILE
7 LINO MELTS

DOWN

1 NICK TIE
2 DIY GIRL
3 ANY IN IT
4 REP DENT

FOUR BY THREE

Can you fit all the letters into the grid to make three four-letter words across and four three-letter words down? We've started you off by placing two of the letters.

A A C̶ E̶ E I
N O R T T T

C			E

JUST A MO

With the help of "MO" in each answer,
can you complete the grid?

M	**O**				
	M	**O**			
		M	**O**		
			M	**O**	
				M	**O**
					M	**O**

1 Gangster
2 Feeling
3 Unethical
4 Din
5 Vacuum flask
6 Sicilian port

THREE THREES

Five nine-lettered words have been randomly split up into three groups of three letters. Can you work out the five words?

TUN	SPA	AWE	GHE	SIA
PEP	UCK	WAR	DYS	AWK
TTI	DLY	STR	ATE	FOR

ANAGRID

Every answer is a word formed from the letters in the clue.

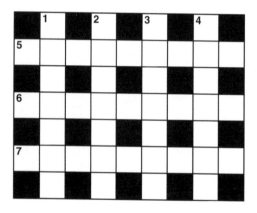

ACROSS
5 BOLD MOSES
6 MICE NOOSE
7 SUET THERE

DOWN
1 COE'S LUG
2 AND SURE
3 RIO, ROME
4 MET OMEN

NO BLANKS!

A crossword with no square wasted!

1	2	3	4
5			
6			
7			
8			
9			

ACROSS
1 Pack tightly
5 Tiny amount
6 Large containers
7 Cut, revise
8 Lose energy
9 Soothsayer

DOWN
1 Asian catlike mammals
2 Pop tour worker
3 Clothe
4 Ship's captain

TAKE FIVE

In this mini crossword, the three answers read the same across and down. We've given you clues to the three words, but not in the right order. See how quickly you can solve it.

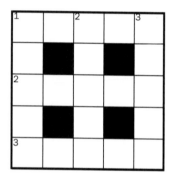

1 Clean and arrange feathers
2 Dutch bulb
3 Fail in virtue or duty

BOX WISE

Can you put these three-letter groups into the numbered boxes to produce twelve six-letter words? Each of them will start in one box and finish in another as indicated by an arrow.

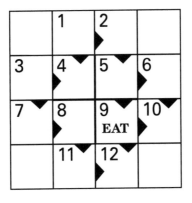

ANA	BAL	BAN
CAB	DER	DIT
EAT	ERY	HER
ING	MEN	MIS

QUICK CROSSWORD

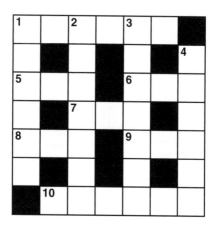

ACROSS
1 Defeated players (6)
5 Mineral spring (3)
6 Two-wheeled carriage (3)
7 By way of (3)
8 Fish eggs (3)
9 Brewer's vat (3)
10 Alternative route (6)

DOWN
1 Not winners (6)
2 Forced labor (7)
3 Yachting event (7)
4 Representatives (6)

ANAGRID

Every answer is a word formed from
the letters in the clue.

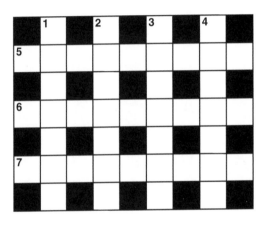

ACROSS
5 GOBI DELTA
6 DARN DOLLS!
7 DANES RULE

DOWN
1 IN BOATS
2 WIRED IN
3 OUR CASE
4 HAD A YEW

FOUR BY THREE

Can you fit all the letters into the grid to make
three four-letter words across and four three-letter words
down? We've started you off by placing one of the letters.

A   B   E   E   F   I
L   N   Ø   O   T   T

	O		

OR-BIT

With the help of "OR" in each answer can you complete the grid?

1	O	R				
2		O	R			
3			O	R		
4				O	R	
5					O	R
6						O	R

1 Neat
2 Asleep
3 Decorated
4 Capers
5 Beg
6 Patron

ANAGRID

Every answer is a new word formed from the letters used in the clue.

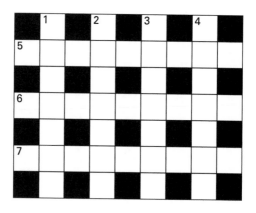

ACROSS
5 TRACE ELBE
6 GENT'S DIET
7 SAP'S GREEN

DOWN
1 NEAR LEG
2 SEE LEAR
3 GIG RANT
4 TINKERS

QUICK CROSSWORD

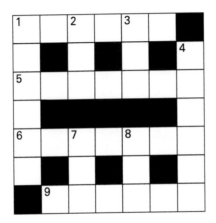

ACROSS
1 Fashion-conscious (6)
5 A thousand thousands (7)
6 Female sovereign (7)
9 Secondary route (6)

DOWN
1 Maiden (6)
2 Snakelike fish (3)
3 Glide over snow (3)
4 As new (6)
7 Snoop (3)
8 The Self (3)

NO BLANKS!

A crossword with no square wasted!

1	2	3	4
5			
6			
7			
8			
9			

ACROSS
1 Sit for a photo
5 Triangle's peak
6 Muck
7 Woman of rank
8 Exclusive British school
9 Bodywork bash

DOWN
1 Made to look bigger
2 Sedative
3 Religious address
4 Scope

SCRAMBLOGRAM

Can you unscramble the six words listed so that the six new words can be placed into the grid? One letter has already been placed to help you on your way.

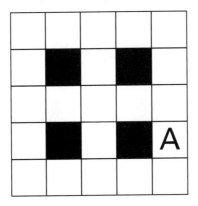

ROUGE   REGAL   SLINK
SLEPT   STRAP   PELTS

QUICK CROSSWORD

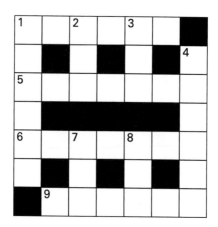

ACROSS

1 Feebly (6)
5 Put back **(7)**
6 Beforehand (7)
9 Except if (6)

DOWN

1 Prison worker (6)
2 Cleopatra's snake (3)
3 Meadowland (3)
4 Scattered wreckage (6)
7 Organized (3)
8 Fury (3)

ANAGRID

Every answer is a word formed from
the letters in the clue.

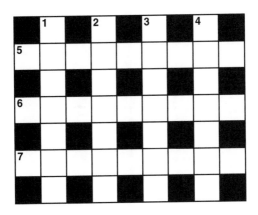

ACROSS
5 CUE AN OGRE
6 RIGHT FONT
7 LATE THROB

DOWN
1 YON DANE
2 OUR STEP
3 STIR TEA
4 HAG EDGE

BOX WISE

Can you put these three-letter groups into the
numbered boxes to produce twelve six-letter words?
Each of them will start in one box and finish
in another as indicated by an arrow.

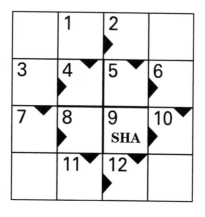

	ANY	BOT	COT
	HER	LAY	MAN
	MAS	SHA	SIL
	TON	WAY	VER

ANAGRID

Every answer is a new word formed from
the letters used in the clue.

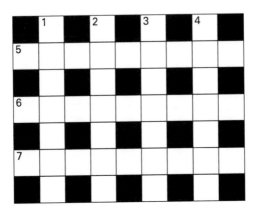

ACROSS
5 LIDO ALARM
6 NO TINY YAM
7 FOR SPORES

DOWN
1 GARY RAN
2 IN MY FAG
3 SID SIMS
4 EAT LION!

ANAGRID

Every answer is a word formed from
the letters in the clue.

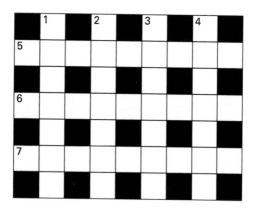

ACROSS

5 AGREE HINT

6 RINGED AGE

7 IS SETTING

DOWN

1 TEA DIVE

2 GIN GERM

3 SO TIRED

4 DISSENT

FOUR BY THREE

Can you fit all the letters into the grid to make three four-letter words across and four three-letter words down? We've started you off by placing two of the letters.

A A E E G
L R S T W W

			A
	W		

OR ELSE!

With the help of "OR" in each answer can you complete the grid?

1	O	R				
2		O	R			
3			O	R		
4				O	R	
5					O	R
6						O	R

1 Fruit grove
2 Proper
3 Spanish sausage
4 Chaperones
5 Looking glasses
6 Pilot

QUICK CROSSWORD

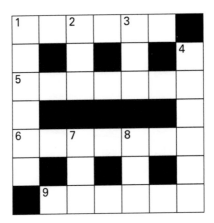

ACROSS
1 Harmony (6)
5 Most baggy (7)
6 Beginning to weaken (7)
9 Concurred (6)

DOWN
1 Permits (6)
2 Dove's cry (3)
3 Cereal grass (3)
4 Theatrically presented (6)
7 Pull with difficulty (3)
8 Skating surface (3)

ANAGRID

Every answer is a new word formed from
the letters used in the clue.

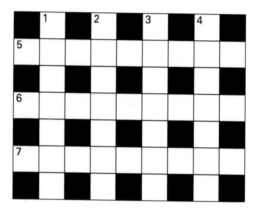

ACROSS

5 TINY DREAM
6 PALE SAILS
7 HORN CREEP

DOWN

1 TRAGEDY
2 CALL FAY
3 DETAILS
4 NO SNIPE

NO BLANKS!

A crossword with no square wasted!

1	2	3	4
5			
6			
7			
8			
9			

ACROSS
1 Big vases
5 Irish fuel?
6 Woman of rank
7 Solo vocal piece
8 Be liable
9 Restive

DOWN
1 Modernize
2 Brought up
3 Designating
4 Reliably firm

QUICK CROSSWORD

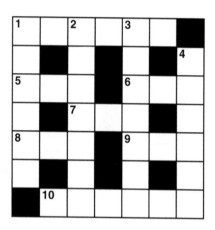

ACROSS

1 Refracting glasses (6)
5 Bushy head of hair (3)
6 Steal from (3)
7 Take food (3)
8 Went first (3)
9 Solid water (3)
10 Casual top (1-5)

DOWN

1 Having acne (6)
2 Obstructs (7)
3 Gin and vermouth cocktail (7)
4 Most competent (6)

ANAGRID

Every answer is a new word formed from
the letters used in the clue.

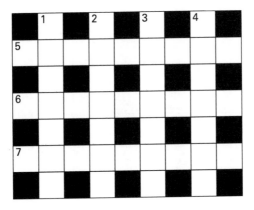

ACROSS
5 FOG ARISES
6 GALLEY LED
7 MUTILATES

DOWN
1 SEA TOIL
2 MAD MILE
3 DRY ROLE
4 GAY TILE

RASPUTIN

With the help of "RAS" in each line,
can you solve all the clues?

1				R	A	S
2			R	A	S	
3		R	A	S		
4	R	A	S			
5	R	A	S			

1 Persian light god
2 Breastplate
3 Sunshade
4 Golf club
5 Mischief makers

QUICK CROSSWORD

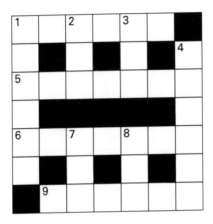

ACROSS

1 How much can one limb hold? (6)
5 Countless (7)
6 Farm vehicle (7)
9 Very determined (6)

DOWN

1 Grown-ups (6)
2 Driver's chart (3)
3 Operate (3)
4 Desktop container (2-4)
7 Play section (3)
8 Golf peg (3)

BOX WISE

Can you put these three-letter groups into the twelve numbered boxes to produce twelve six-letter words, each of which starts in one box and finishes in another as indicated by an arrow?

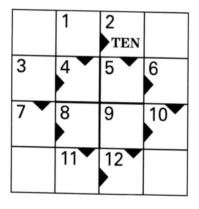

	1	2	
		▶TEN	
3	4 ▼	5 ▼	6
7 ▼	8	9	10 ▼
	11 ▼	12 ▼	

COT   DRA   IAN
ICS   INS   ION
MAS   MED   PIN
PLA   TEN   TON

BE-BOP

With the help of "BE" in each answer,
can you complete the grid?

1 As well as
2 Following orders
3 Freedom
4 Floating hazard
5 Knifed
6 Attribute

QUICK CROSSWORD

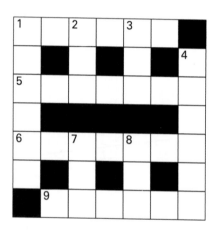

ACROSS
1 Strong commendation (6)
5 Turn aside (7)
6 On the way out? (7)
9 Add on (6)

DOWN
1 Go in ankle deep! (6)
2 Alien living with the Tanners (3)
3 That lady (3)
4 Theatrically presented (6)
7 Small snake (3)
8 Fury (3)

TO TRUE

With the help of "TO" in each answer,
can you complete the grid?

	T	O				
1	T	O				
2		T	O			
3			T	O		
4				T	O	
5					T	O
6						T	O

ACROSS
1 Smokers' plant
2 Making amends
3 Amaze

DOWN
4 Animated film
5 Pilot
6 Souvenir

SHADY BUSINESS

Can you fit the listed words into the grid?
If you can, a nine-letter word will appear in the shaded squares.
What is it?

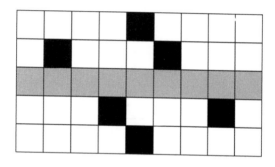

3	4	5
AGE	NEWS	MANSE
APE	OMEN	NESTS
ATE	SKUA	SIGHT
EGG	TEST	USERS
ENS		
HER		
INN		
REE		
SPA		

QUICK CROSSWORD

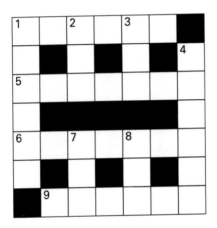

ACROSS
1 Fearful cry (6)
5 ___ Christie, sprinter (7)
6 Hole for a tenon (7)
9 Protest (6)

DOWN
1 Highly seasoned sausage (6)
2 Smuggle (3)
3 Clamor (3)
4 Most peculiar (6)
7 Chafe (3)
8 Skating surface (3)

BY THE BY

With the help of "BY" in each answer,
can you complete the grid?

						B	Y
1						B	Y
2					B	Y	
3				B	Y		
4			B	Y			
5		B	Y				
6	B	Y					

1 Australian marsupial
2 Adieu
3 Tots' word for "goodbye"
4 Infantile
5 Really bad
6 Interesting old things

NO BLANKS!

A crossword with no square wasted!

1	2	3	4
5			
6			
7			
8			
9			

ACROSS
1 Pulpy substances
5 On top of
6 Type of parasitic insect
7 Dwarf pug-dog
8 Maple tree
9 Allows

DOWN
1 Type of tooth abscess
2 Per person
3 Cavity, found in clothes
4 Scoffs

QUICK CROSSWORD

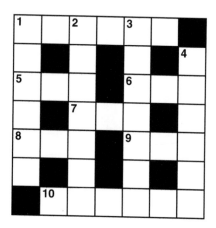

ACROSS
1 Scottish musicians (6)
5 Adult male (3)
6 Boxlike vehicle (3)
7 Glide across snow (3)
8 T'ai ___, martial art (3)
9 Bird reputed to be wise (3)
10 Inviting (6)

DOWN
1 Lava used as a cleaning stone (6)
2 Flowers of the viola family (7)
3 Meat-filled pasta cases (7)
4 Remove a blockage (6)

FOUR BY THREE

Can you fit all the letters into the grid to make three four-letter words across and four three-letter words down? We've started you off by placing two of the letters.

A ~~A~~ D D E I
M N ~~N~~ O R T

	A		
		N	

LO AND BEHOLD

With the help of "LO" in each answer,
can you complete the grid?

	L	O				
1	L	O				
2		L	O			
3			L	O		
4				L	O	
5					L	O
6					L	O

1 Detested
2 Puffed-up
3 Let
4 Unfeeling
5 Kept men
6 Little flute

QUICK CROSSWORD

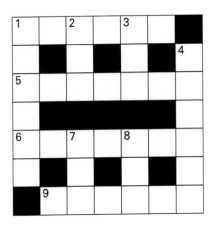

ACROSS

1 Haggle (6)
5 Comes into view (7)
6 Misshapen (7)
9 Official head count (6)

DOWN

1 Subsidiary outlet (6)
2 Rend (3)
3 Historical period (3)
4 Audience-only remarks? (6)
7 Source mineral (3)
8 Greek island off the Turkish coast (3)

NO BLANKS!

A crossword with no square wasted!

1	2	3	4
5			
6			
7			
8			
9			

ACROSS
1 Stare in amazement
5 Opera song
6 Charts
7 Wading bird
8 Square root of 81
9 Stage jokes

DOWN
1 Casino activity
2 Saudi ___, Mecca's country
3 Cleaning off
4 Exceeds

BOX WISE

Can you put these three-letter groups into the numbered boxes to produce twelve six-letter words? Each of them will start in one box and finish in another as indicated by an arrow.

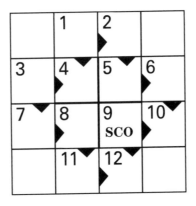

	1 ▶	2 ▶	
3	4 ▶	5 ▶	6 ▶
7 ▶	8 ▶	9 SCO ▶	10 ▶
	11 ▶	12 ▶	

ENT	FER	HER
MIT	PER	RAP
RED	REG	RET
RIC	SCO	USE

•SOLUTIONS•

SOLUTIONS

Page 6

Page 7

Page 8

Page 9

Page 10

Page 11

Page 12

Page 13

Page 14

Page 15

Page 16

The missing letter is W

SOLUTIONS

Page 17

ODDJOB
A U A
SONIC
H I K
IMPEL
N E O
GARAGE

Page 18

PAW BID
O A I O
TAXABLE
T E
EACHWAY
R O I E
YEW GAD

Page 19

GRASS
B U L
WINEBOX
C W
UKELELE
E A Y
FROWN

Page 20

T I
ROADHOG
O U I N
UNDERGO
N I E B
CITADEL
E E

Page 21

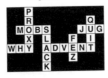

P
R
MOBS JUG
X F I
WHY ADVENT
A Z
C
K

Page 22

IMAGE
O E C
SCALLOP
K G
SULTANS
P O A
COUCH

Page 23

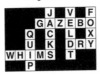

J V F
GAZEBO
Q C L X
U K DRY
WHIMS T
P

The missing letter is N

Page 24

REBUILD
H E R A
USE KEY
B L
ASS AGO
R E S N
BEARHUG

Page 25

T
FINANCE
T L L
SLEEPIN
E R P
EDITION
N

Page 26

PASTRY
E P E
WHIPPY
N R
ADJOIN
L O I
EYEFUL

SOLUTIONS

Page 27

Page 28

Page 29

Page 30

Page 31

Page 32

The missing letter is P

Page 33

Page 34

Page 35

Page 36

SOLUTIONS

Page 37

Page 38

The missing letter is V

Page 39

Page 40

Page 41

Page 42

Page 43

Page 44

Page 45

Page 46

Page 47

119

SOLUTIONS

Page 48

```
M . B . . L
G O D F A T H E R
W . . C K . V
. J . . . Y
Q U I P S
. N . . .
. X
```

The missing letter is Z

Page 49

```
F A N C I E D
R . I . N . A
O R B . K E Y
S . . . . . L
T U B . A G O
E . U . I . N
D I S H R A G
```

Page 50

```
W E B . S O B
A . U . K . I
D A N C I N G . O
D . . . . . O
I N B U I L T
N . U . L . E
G E T . K I D
```

Page 51

```
. M O C H A
. W . U . U
A I R T I M E
. N . . M
S T I C K U P
. E . O . S
D R A P E
```

Page 52

```
S . . . . C
M O R O C C O
A . O . H . R
R E T H I N K
T . O . L . A
E A R P L U G
N . . . . E
```

Page 53

```
R A S C A L
A . E . S . P
F E A T H E R
T . . . . I
E F F A C E S
R . O . O . O
T E N D O N
```

Page 54

```
A T T E N T I O N
R . P . I . P
M O M E N T O U S
W . R . A . L
M E R G A N S E R
L . N . I . N
E S P E R A N T O
```

Page 55

```
A . V . A . S
I M P E N D I N G
N . R . V . I
H E A D L A N D S
S . U . N . E
M I C R O C O S M
A . E . E . T
```

Page 56

```
F E L L
A R I A
C A L M
I S L E
N E I L
G R E Y
```

Page 57

```
D E F A M E
I . L . A . D
V I E . R O E
E . E A T . S
R O C . I M P
T . E . N . O
. T S H I R T
```

Page 58

```
1 CON  2 DOR
3 PRE  4 FAB  5 MER  6 LIN
7 STO  8 LES  9 CER  10 EAL
11 ION 12 ISE
```

120

SOLUTIONS

Page 59

	S	O		H		G
E	P	I	S	C	O	P	A	L
U		T		S		V
I	T	E	R	A	T	I	O	N
T		I		I		T
P	E	R	C	O	L	A	T	E
R		H		E		E

Page 60

S	T	A	L	E	M	A	T	E
E		O		A		A
I	M	P	O	R	T	U	N	E
P		K		I		G
R	E	S	O	U	N	D	E	D
S		U		E		N
S	T	A	T	U	E	T	T	E

Page 61

C	H	O	O	S	E
A		H		K		A
L	E	M	M	I	N	G
L						R
O	B	V	I	A	T	E
W		A		R		E
	S	C	A	M	P	S

Page 62

S	O	R	C	E	R	Y
I	S	O	L	A	T	E
M	A	S	O	N	R	Y
E	Y	E	S	O	R	E
A	E	R	O	S	O	L
C	A	L	Y	P	S	O

Page 63

T	U	M	B	L	E
H		A		E		B
R	E	T	I	N	U	E
O						A
W	I	E	L	D	E	D
N		M		O		L
	B	U	S	T	L	E

Page 64

A		A		S		M
T	R	I	P	L	A	N	E	S
T		P		T		D
C	I	N	E	M	A	T	I	C
C		A		N		A
A	L	A	R	M	I	S	T	S
E		S		C		E

Page 65

1 Starlit

2 Utility

3 Militia

4 Glitter

5 Liturgy

Page 66

	D		D		D		G
S	E	M	I	F	I	N	A	L
B		S		G		L
C	A	M	P	A	N	I	L	E
T		O		I		E
T	E	R	R	I	T	O	R	Y
R		T		Y		Y

Page 67

F	A	C	E
I	B	E	X
B	R	A	T
B	A	S	E
E	D	E	N
R	E	S	T

Page 68

Page 69

S	C	U	R	R	Y
U		S		A		M
B	E	A	S	T	L	Y
B						S
E	N	H	A	N	C	E
D		E		F		L
	E	N	G	U	L	F

Page 70

	K		R		I		P
V	I	S	I	O	N	A	R	Y
N		G		A		E
G	E	L	I	G	N	I	T	E
T		D		I		E
M	I	L	L	S	T	O	N	E
C		Y		Y		D

SOLUTIONS

Page 71

C	O	T	E
A	R	I	A
T	E	N	T

Page 72

M	O	B	S	T	E	R
E	M	O	T	I	O	N
I	M	M	O	R	A	L
A	N	E	M	O	N	E
T	H	E	R	M	O	S
P	A	L	E	R	M	O

Page 73

1 Awestruck
2 Spaghetti
3 Dyspepsia
4 Fortunate
5 Awkwardly

Page 74

Page 75

C	R	A	M
I	O	T	A
V	A	T	S
E	D	I	T
T	I	R	E
S	E	E	R

Page 76

1 (2) Tulip
2 (3) Lapse
3 (1) Preen

Page 77

Page 78

Page 79

Page 80

F	O	A	L
I	N	T	O
B	E	E	T

Page 81

O	R	D	E	R	L	Y
D	O	R	M	A	N	T
A	D	O	R	N	E	D
C	A	V	O	R	T	S
I	M	P	L	O	R	E
S	P	O	N	S	O	R

Page 82

SOLUTIONS

Page 83

D	R	E	S	S	Y
A		E		K		U
M	I	L	L	I	O	N
S						U
E	M	P	R	E	S	S
L		R		G		E
	B	Y	R	O	A	D

Page 84

P	O	S	E
A	P	E	X
D	I	R	T
D	A	M	E
E	T	O	N
D	E	N	T

Page 85

K	A	R	T	S
I		O		P
L	A	G	E	R
N		U		A
S	L	E	P	T

Page 86

W	E	A	K	L	Y	
A		S		E		D
R	E	P	L	A	C	E
D						B
E	A	R	L	I	E	R
N		A		R		I
	U	N	L	E	S	S

Page 87

	A		P		A		E	
E	N	C	O	U	R	A	G	E
	N		S		T		A	
F	O	R	T	N	I	G	H	T
	Y		U		S		E	
B	E	T	R	O	T	H	A	L
	D		E		E		D	

Page 88

	1 MAS	2 COT	
3 BOT	4 HER	5 TON	6 SIL
7 ANY	8 WAY	9 SHA	10 VER
	11 LAY	12 MAN	

Page 89

	G		M	D		E	
A	R	M	A	D	I	L	L	O
	A		G		S		A	
A	N	O	N	Y	M	I	T	Y
	A		I		I		I	
P	R	O	F	E	S	S	O	R
	Y		Y		S		N	

Page 90

	D		M	S		S	
R	E	H	E	A	T	I	N	G
	V		R		E		E	
G	I	N	G	E	R	A	D	E
	A		I		O		E	
S	T	I	N	G	I	E	S	T
	E		G		D		T	

Page 91

S	A	G	A
E	W	E	R
W	E	L	T

Page 92

O	R	C	H	A	R	D
C	O	R	R	E	C	T
C	H	O	R	I	Z	O
E	S	C	O	R	T	S
M	I	R	R	O	R	S
A	V	I	A	T	O	R

Page 93

A	C	C	O	R	D	
L		O		Y		S
L	O	O	S	E	S	T
O						A
W	I	L	T	I	N	G
S		U		C		E
	A	G	R	E	E	D

123

SOLUTIONS

Page 94

G		F		D		P	
D	Y	N	A	M	I	T	E	R
R		L		L		N	
P	A	L	L	I	A	S	S	E
T		A		T		I	
P	E	R	C	H	E	R	O	N
D		Y		S		N	

Page 95

U	R	N	S
P	E	A	T
D	A	M	E
A	R	I	A
T	E	N	D
E	D	G	Y

Page 96

P	R	I	S	M	S	
I		M		A		A
M	O	P		R	O	B
P		E	A	T		L
L	E	D		I	C	E
Y		E		N		S
	T	S	H	I	R	T

Page 97

	I		D		O		E	
O	S	S	I	F	R	A	G	E
	O		L		D		A	
A	L	L	E	G	E	D	L	Y
	A		M		R		I	
S	T	I	M	U	L	A	T	E
	E		A		Y		Y	

Page 98

1 Mithras
2 Cuirass
3 Parasol
4 Brassie
5 Rascals

Page 99

A	R	M	F	U	L	
D		A		S		I
U	M	P	T	E	E	N
L						T
T	R	A	C	T	O	R
S		C		E		A
	S	T	E	E	L	Y

Page 100

Page 101

B	E	S	I	D	E	S
O	B	E	Y	I	N	G
L	I	B	E	R	T	Y
I	C	E	B	E	R	G
S	T	A	B	B	E	D
A	S	C	R	I	B	E

Page 102

P	R	A	I	S	E	
A		L		H		S
D	E	F	L	E	C	T
D						A
L	E	A	V	I	N	G
E		S		R		E
	A	P	P	E	N	D

Page 103

T	O	B	A	C	C	O
A	T	O	N	I	N	G
A	S	T	O	U	N	D
C	A	R	T	O	O	N
A	V	I	A	T	O	R
M	E	M	E	N	T	O

Page 104

S	K	U	A		O	M	E	N
I		S	P	A		A	G	E
G	R	E	E	T	I	N	G	S
H	E	R		E	N	S		T
T	E	S	T			N	E	W	S

SOLUTIONS

Page 105

S	C	R	E	A	M	
A		U		D		O
L	I	N	F	O	R	D
A						D
M	O	R	T	I	S	E
I		U		C		S
	O	B	J	E	C	T

Page 106

W	A	L	L	A	B	Y
G	O	O	D	B	Y	E
B	Y	E	B	Y	E	S
B	A	B	Y	I	S	H
A	B	Y	S	M	A	L
B	Y	G	O	N	E	S

Page 107

P	A	P	S
U	P	O	N
L	I	C	E
P	E	K	E
A	C	E	R
L	E	T	S

Page 108

P	I	P	E	R	S	
U		A		A		U
M	A	N		V	A	N
I		S	K	I		C
C	H	I		O	W	L
E		E		L		O
	A	S	K	I	N	G

Page 109

D	A	T	A
I	R	O	N
M	E	N	D

Page 110

L	O	A	T	H	E	D
B	L	O	A	T	E	D
A	L	L	O	W	E	D
C	A	L	L	O	U	S
G	I	G	O	L	O	S
P	I	C	C	O	L	O

Page 111

B	A	R	T	E	R	
R		I		R		A
A	P	P	E	A	R	S
N						I
C	R	O	O	K	E	D
H		R		O		E
	C	E	N	S	U	S

Page 112

G	A	W	P
A	R	I	A
M	A	P	S
I	B	I	S
N	I	N	E
G	A	G	S

Page 113

125

PUZZLE NOTES

PUZZLE NOTES

PUZZLE NOTES

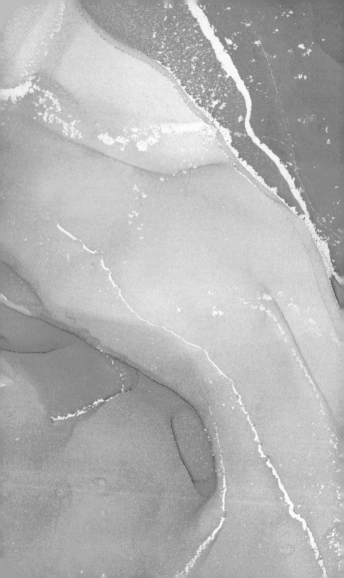